PAIN to PURPOSE

A Short Story with a Big Impact

Dr. DaMesia Starling

www.selfpublishn30days.com

Published by *Self Publish -N- 30 Days*

Copyright 2020 Dr. DaMesia Starling

All rights reserved worldwide. No part of this book may be reproduced or transmitted in any form or by any means electronic or mechanical, including photocopying, recording or by any information storage and retrieval system without written permission from Dr. DaMesia Starling.

Printed in the United States of America

ISBN: 979-8-61780-021-2

1. Autobiography 2. Inspirational 3. Christian 6. Healing

Dr. DaMesia Starling   *Pain to Purpose*

Disclaimer/Warning:

This book is intended for lecture and informative purposes only. This publication is designed to provide competent and reliable information regarding the subject matter covered. The author or publisher are not engaged in rendering legal or professional advice. Laws vary from state to state and if legal, financial, or other expert assistance is needed, the services of a professional should be sought. The author and publisher disclaim any liability that is incurred from the use or application of the contents of this book.

DEDICATION

To my late parents, John L. and Brenda Starling, thank you for loving me unconditionally. Thank you for allowing me to be my own person. Thank you for raising me in a loving and stable environment. I credit you for all of my life's accomplishments and blessings. Not a day goes by that I do not think of you.

My heart aches and rejoices at the same time when I think of you. I wish you both were still here, yet, I know you are in a much better place resting with Jesus. It is my desire to strive daily to make you proud and leave a legacy that would honor you both. The love I know you had for me keeps me going daily. I love you and miss you both dearly.

Love Eternally,

Your baby girl,

Dr. DaMesia D. Starling

Kesia, my one and only sister. It hurts so bad to even type that you are gone. I miss you. I love you. I did everything I knew to do to keep you here with me. I can rest assured knowing you are with Momma and Daddy smiling down on me wondering, what I will do next. I pray you are satisfied with the care I was able to provide for you in the last years of your life. No more sickness, no more medicine, no more pain.

I see your smile through my tears as I type. I knew you loved me and were proud to be my big sister, it showed through your smile whenever you saw me walk in your room to visit you or take you for the weekend. After Momma and Daddy left, you were my world. It was Kesia and Mesia. I was devasted to let you go.. But, I had to. Continue to rest Sister. I love you forever.

ACKNOWLEDGEMENTS

Thank you to my friends and family that have and are continuing to pray for me daily. Your prayers are much appreciated and needed, I am truly grateful for the support I have been given throughout the years.

Thank you.

To my wonderful publisher, Darren M. Palmer, thank you for seeing my vision and assisting me in making my dream of writing my life's story a reality. To my fearless editor Charli Caraway, thank you for EVERYTHING! Thank you for your advice, encouragement, accountability, and open availability. You are simply awesome!

To my best friends, Yalanda Woolridge and Natasha Gross. Thank you. I cannot say thank you enough! Thank you for your shoulders when I needed to cry. Thank you for your listening ear when I needed to vent. Thank you for being present when I needed you the most. You both knew what to say or sometimes what not to say. Thank you. You are my sisters, you are my "people", you are my best friends. I love you both.

TABLE OF CONTENTS

1   Promising- /ˈpräməsiNG/..........................1

2   Pain- /pān/ 7

3   Prayer- /prer/ 15

4   Prevailing- /priˈvāliNG/ 21

5   Perseverance- /pərˈsistəns/ 27

6   Peaceful- /ˈpēsfəl/ 33

7   Purpose- /ˈpərpəs/.................................39

8   Perspective- /pərˈspektiv/......................43

Chapter 1
PROMISING
{ *adjective*. showing signs of future success. }

My Life …

I grew up in a very close-knit family. My parents loved to host holidays, Sunday dinners, and summer barbeques. I could not ask for a more perfect childhood. Reflecting back, I smile, spending the summers with my grandparents and cousins, family dinners, and gatherings were nothing but love and laughter. As a child, I would "play school" with my dolls, mocking my favorite teachers, not knowing one day I would have the honor to touch and mold young lives as well. I was a happy child, loved family and felt a sense of comfort when we were all together. I was truly blessed with the life I was given.

All my needs and wants were met and provided by my parents. My family used to say that I, the last child of John and Brenda Starling, was destined to be a singer. I loved to sing and would make a song out of anything, annoying everyone else, I am sure. My happy childhood led to a promising life. There was never a doubt that I would do great things. I just did not know what those things would be or how I would obtain those "great things." I just knew those great things would happen. During school, I made lots of friends and lived a normal teenage life, having sleepovers, going to the mall, and enjoying the friendships that I made.

Professional Aspirations ...

At the completion of high school, I decided to go to college so I could major in nursing. I also wanted to audition and become a member of the college chorale, which was a very prestigious choir that traveled all over the world. During my initial year in college, I decided to change my major to Education. I knew early on that I wanted to be a teacher, but everyone said nursing was the career to choose if I wanted to maximize in salary ranges. I then transferred colleges where I majored in Education with a minor in Reading.

After graduating college and obtaining a bachelor's degree, I began my teaching career and taught for seven years before returning to graduate school to attain my master's degree in Educational Leadership concentrating on Curriculum, Instruction, and Assessment. After completing 10 successful years of teaching, I decided to transition to education administration. I then became an Assistant Principal and served students, teachers, parents, and the community in that capacity for two years.

I was then afforded the opportunity to become the Principal and Education Director for an all-male prison. During that role, I was able to assist the inmates in obtaining their GEDs and provide counseling and direction for post release employment options.

I then returned to an independent school district setting as a District Coordinator. After serving one year in the role of District Coordinator, I had finally completed my Doctor of Education degree after five long years of hard work. After completing my terminal degree, it was always my hope to transition to higher education. Not knowing what God had in store, I searched for a job in higher education, knowing it would be difficult to acquire such a job with no previous experience at the tertiary level.

I prayed and was consistent in completing higher education job applications, even landing interviews for principal roles and other district positions in the interim. However, my faith was strong, believing I would land a job at a college or university. Deep in my heart, I knew what I wanted to achieve and I was on a mission to be a college professor.

Fall 2018 was quickly approaching and I was feeling down and discouraged because I knew all colleges would be starting classes soon. I had become content, but not satisfied, with the idea that I would return to a school district that Fall. I was reminded that all things happen in God's timing. Although I had a personal timeline expectation for obtaining a college position, God had another plan. One week after classes started, I obtained a position as Director of Student Teaching and Field Experiences/Assistant Professor of Education at my alma mater Jarvis Christian College. I was overjoyed! This was another testimony. Truly, when Jesus says, "Yes," nobody can say, "No!"

Elevation ...

After serving one semester in the role of Assistant Professor/Director of Student Teaching and Field Experiences, I was promoted to Interim Dean of the Division of Education and serve in that role currently. This new role has provided me the opportunity to not only teach future educators and share my experiences with them, but I am able to build relationships and be a mentor for the students I reach daily.

On May 4, 2019, I participated in the first commencement ceremony as Interim Dean of Education. As I sat on the same stage that I crossed 16 years prior to receive my bachelor's degree, I thought to myself, "God, you are amazing and I truly thank you." I reflected that 16 years ago, I would not have imagined sitting here or even doing the things that He was blessing me to do. All the hard work and late nights of doing homework, writing papers, and reading articles paid off. I am presented with opportunities to travel and meet fellow colleagues in the field of higher education to learn from them and network.

I can honestly say that God has truly blessed me. Although, I have worked very hard to obtain the academic accolades I have received, God continues to elevate me in my career. God truly surpassed my expectations with the blessings He has given me. There were times when I did not feel I was good enough and I now know that pain and sorrow is not all I am.

Through all the trials and hurdles I have encountered, I never had a doubt that God would lead me to higher heights. I am excited to see where God will lead me next.

As this chapter ends, I wanted to share the scripture that helped me get through difficult times, knowing that God's promises are true. Isaiah 40:31 helped me see the light in the darkness I experienced. Please reflect and share how and what helped you make it to see that God's promises are true.

Reflection
PERSONAL PROMISES

Chapter 2
PAIN

{ *noun*. physical suffering or mental discomfort caused by illness or injury. }

Growing up in a family that was close was wonderful. I was the youngest child, with an older sister and an older step-brother that lives in Houston. I would love Friday nights as a child. That was our night to go out to eat as a family and then go visit my grandparents. Those were the best of times, being able to play with my cousins and just be around family. I can recall Sundays after church, playing in my grandmother's yard with my cousins enjoying being young and carefree. But by the age of 30, my life changed.

My dad became ill and passed away in May of 2008. Losing him was a void I cannot explain. My heart broke for the first time. The loss of a loved one is a feeling that no words can describe. The mere fact that I would never talk to my dad, hear his loud laugh, laugh at his jokes, or eat his delicious barbeque again was unimaginable. Yet it became my present reality. I had comfort in knowing he was not suffering in pain anymore, but my heart wanted and needed him on Earth. As life slowly became "normal" again a year later, my heart broke for the second time.

My mom passed away suddenly in December of 2009. I often thought, could life be this cruel twice? Obviously so. This was my reality. My parents are now gone. How could this be happening? How am I supposed to go through life as "nobody's little girl"? My heart, my soul, my being had changed completely and no one could possibly understand the pain I felt. I still had my sister and I knew I had to pick up the pieces to continue to live and support her.

Although I was the youngest, I was the sole supporter of my sister in every aspect. My sister was my mother's shadow, when you saw my mother, you saw my sister. My sister was not independent enough to live alone or on her own. At this point, it was only my sister and me. So, I knew I had to step up and ensure that she had what she needed. Yes, she was older by 5 years, but I had always acted as if I was older. I thank God, I had a career and could provide for her and myself. We still had each other. Life has a way of providing strength and eventually, I had a new normal.

A couple years after the death of my mother, my sister became seriously ill. She spent weeks in ICU unresponsive. Again, I asked, "Can life be this damn cruel? What is happening here? Why is this happening?" These were my thoughts. Days and nights passed and I watched my sister fight for her life. I am thankful for family and friends that prayed for me and with me, brought food to the hospital, sat with me while I was at the hospital. I was grateful to be surrounded by love and pure support.

After praying, waiting and wondering, my sister finally regained consciousness. There was a relief inside me like never before. I KNEW she would come through. She HAD to. I kept thinking, "Christmas is next week." This cannot be happening. Slowly, doctors would tell me all the ailments that my sister had. I could not care for her properly with me teaching full time. She needed around-the-clock care. I had to make the second-hardest decision in my life. The first was taking my mother off life support, and now I had to make the choice to place my only sister in a skilled nursing facility.

Pain

Again, my chest hurt. Pain returned. Why, Lord? She is ALL I have and I must put her in a home? I couldn't understand why my life had so many pitfalls. Like before, life has a way of making us resilient. After the initial pain and separation anxiety subsided, my life once again took on a "new normal".

After a year, I moved my sister to a better facility and she quickly began to improve and was able to come home with me on weekends and for family events. I was thankful each time I saw her improve and slowly return to her old self, piece by piece. I was able to regain myself and not worry about her as much. With each day, I thanked God. Then on Tuesday, January 17, 2017, my heart broke for the third time. I got a call. My sister had passed away.

I had no words. Why? I couldn't take anymore. My heart was broken in a million pieces. On that rainy day, my best friend came to pick me up from work because I was in no shape to drive. I was in shock, but I had no tears yet. I just kept thinking, "Lord, why?" As I walked into the hospital and was lead to the room where my sister was, I could see my family sitting, some standing … but everything was a blur, moving fast yet slow. The doctors came to talk to me, telling me they did all they could. I heard the words but couldn't quite grasp them. As the doctors talked, I was thinking, "Is this happening? Am I alone? Yes. I. Am. Alone. I have no family. Really?"

As they opened the door to the room where my sister was, I stood there and saw her lying on the bed. Looking as if she was asleep. I saw the torn dress, as if the doctors were in a haste to save her. Yet, to no avail. She was gone. I grabbed her cold hands. I was thinking, "My sister is gone. Wow." I rubbed her face and closed her eyes as one was still open.

At this point, I began to shake. I got cold as if a strong wind had come into the room. I then was approached by a hospital official asking me which funeral home they should call. The words resonated in my mind, as I had heard them two times prior. I uttered the information requested. I asked my family to stay as my sister was taken to the morgue. I couldn't bear to see her in that bag being rolled out. I asked my best friend to take me home. I wanted to leave. I just wanted to go. I went home to try to understand what had become of my life. I was so broken.

My new normal was a very difficult adjustment. After losing my parents, my primary focus was school, work, and ensuring my sister was taken care of.Initially, when my sister passed away, it was very difficult not going by the nursing home or calling my sister's cell phone to see what she needed me to bring her that week. I would go see her at least three times a week and do her laundry on the weekends. That was her time to request any needed hygiene and personal items she needed. I must admit, there were times that I became frustrated and often thought how unfair my life was. But when those thoughts came, I would think about my sister and remember, I am all she has and I must make sure she is okay and receiving proper care.My constant thought and prayer was to ensure my sister knew I would never leave her and I was going to take care of her.

As days turned into weeks, and weeks turned into months, and months turned into years, the voids in my life were unbearable. Holidays are the worst. Holidays are a time where family unites and gets together to laugh, fellowship, and have fun. Holidays for me for a while included lying in bed all day with my phone turned off, dealing with the sick feeling I had inside my stomach.

One thing I did not do was feel sorry for myself. Abandonment was definitely a feeling that came over me quite often. Although I have plenty of aunts, uncles, cousins, and friends, they do not compare to having my parents and

Pain

my sister here with me. I would see people with their moms, dads, or even just family in general and I would instantly feel jealous. I wanted that back. I wanted the feeling of going to my parents' house to visit, have dinner, and take a nap in my childhood room. I just wanted do the things most take for granted. I always knew that God had a reason for everything I was going through. Even all these years later, I don't understand His plan, but I do know I want to transcend my pain into purpose.

Revelation 21:4 reminds me that God will wipe away all my tears. Weeping may endure for a night, but joy comes in the morning. When pain comes, it is okay to cry, but know that God is a great comforter.

Reflection
PERSONAL PAINS

Share your favorite Bible verse that helped you cope with pain, a loss, or overall depression.

Chapter 3
PRAYER

{ *noun.* a solemn request for help or expression of thanks addressed to God or an object of worship. }

Prayer is an opportunity to spend time with God. To really understand the heart of God, you need to pray. In John 15:15, Jesus says He no longer calls us His servants, but calls us His friends. Talking with God develops a deeper relationship with Him. It's impossible to know someone if you don't spend time with them.

Prayer has always been a constant in my life growing up through adulthood. As life's hurdles became harder for me to climb over, I knew early on that I would not be able to make it through any of them without my higher power. Prayer got me through the most difficult times in my life. I KNOW without a doubt somebody, somewhere is STILL praying for me.

I often sit and think about the things that God has allowed me to overcome, the things that I have gone through, the barriers and hurdles I have climbed over with triumph. Nobody but God has kept me. I have shared my story with a few people and the immediate reaction from them is "How do you still smile?" My response is always, "Someone is praying for me." I could not and would not be able to be who I am today, sound mind and body without the prayers of the righteous.

During times of prosperity, my prayers were of thanksgiving and reflection, being thankful for the blessings God had blessed me with and reflecting on the path I have taken in life. I thank God daily for the many blessings that I am fortunate to have. I have the ability to live an overcomer mindset; wanting to continue to advance in life, after it has thrown me so many curve balls. I was determined to be the best version of myself and not let my circumstances define who I am. It was prayer that continued to keep me strong, it was prayer that kept me strong physically and mentally. I thank God for all the prayers that were prayed for me and my well-being.

I won't say that I do not have those moments that hurt so bad that it literally takes the breath out of me. Those moments never come with a sign or warning. I can be fine one moment, the next, I feel tears flowing down my face. There is no explaining the deep wanting to hear your mom's voice, see the smile of your sister, and hear your dad call your name. It hurts. Once you accept this is your life, your reality, there comes a pain in the pit of your stomach that is strong enough to knock you to your knees. In those moments, all I can do is whisper this prayer, "Jesus, help me, please give me strength." Those words provide strength and comfort.

Sometimes we forget how powerful prayer is. The power of prayer is so great it has the power to defeat the devil and his power over us. He wants to destroy us, but God wants to bring us closer to Him. Prayer is our tool to win that battle. Prayer gives us the strength and the faith to finish the race victorious.

At a young age I was taught to pray. I grew up in church and was very active singing in the choir, serving as an usher, and participating in various church activities. Even now, I pray daily. Prayer is the key to enduring all the worry and stress the world may present. God does not expect me to know it all, have it all together, or do it all. I now know He just wants me to trust Him through it all.

Prayer

I sit and reflect on my life and how God continues to cover me with his love, favor, mercy, and grace. I know prayers of many helped me stay strong for the most part. Even to this day, my friends tell me, they sent up prayers during holidays, birthdays, and/or the anniversaries of the deaths of my family members.

I am most thankful for my friends. Without them, my grieving process would have been much harder than what it has been. But through the healing process, I realized that I could not constantly call them whenever I was feeling sad or down. I learned that when I did so, I inadvertently made them sad because my family was just like their family.

To date, my friends continue to encourage me to discuss my feelings with them and not keep things bottled inside or try to deal with things myself. I have learned to call and rely on them for support when I feel that I just can't handle the weight of grief and the unbearable sadness it brings. Although I have a strong support system, during those difficult times, prayer is my primary source of relief and a constant way for me to have inner peace and strength.

I have gained courage through dealing with the life that was designed for me. Losing both parents and my only sister definitely made me become an adult. I gained the mindset of having to succeed and make sure I have the best life I can despite the hurdles I have had to climb.

Through every death, every funeral I have had to plan, to every tombstone I have had to design, I have grown. I had two choices, let my situations kill me and my spirit, or stay close to God and trust His will for my life to continue to strive to be the best version of myself.

When I feel that my prayers are not enough, I can always refer to Psalm 34:18 to provide that additional confirmation.

Reflection
PERSONAL PRAYER ROUTINE

Share your favorite Bible verse that helped you strengthen your prayer life.

_____
_____
_____
_____
_____
_____
_____
_____
_____
_____
_____
_____
_____

Chapter 4
PREVAILING

{ *adjective*. existing at a particular time; current. }

I have always had the attitude that failure is not an option. Going through the storms that life has presented to me, I could have easily gone into a dark place. Yet, with each storm faced, I prayed through the dark days because I knew that the sun would shine again. I didn't know when, but, I knew it would. I would smile when my heart was breaking. I do believe my faith in God sustained me. Growing up in church, I was taught that God would never put more on you than you can bear. I was not going to let what I had gone through define me or my future.

I continued to teach after the death of my dad, eventually starting my master's program in 2008, not knowing that before I received my master's, I would be planning a funeral for my mother. I had some dark moments after losing my mother and moving my sister into a nursing facility. However, I knew I had to stay strong for my sister and myself, which was sometimes tough, but again, that's where prayer became my source of strength.

In 2013, I decided to challenge myself yet again and applied to Walden University's Doctoral program. Once I began the Doctoral program, I was not aware of the time and dedication it would take to remain on top of the course load. Deadlines and papers were a constant, which left little time for anything other than reading, writing, and researching. However, I learned to bring balance into my weekly routines, over time, and I realized that I must have at least one day to do something I enjoyed which excluded writing, reading, and research.

As I got closer to completing my doctoral journey, I was excited and filled with a sense of accomplishment. Not knowing that in 2017 just months before graduating with my doctorate, I would be planning my sister's funeral.

A will to do more than just exist was strong within me. I knew my situation would not define me, I wouldn't allow it to. I never stopped believing that great things would happen in my life, even with all the bad I had experienced. I knew God had bigger things in store for me. Although I wanted to quit and crawl into a corner, I allowed tears to fall down my face many, many times, but I wiped them and said, "Okay, what's next?"

I can remember being up late working on my dissertation, conducting research, and reading articles and out of the blue, tears would well in my eyes. I would find myself crying, sometimes a few tears would fall, and other times, the ugly cry would happen. The pain would come from no point in particular, but it happened and I had to release it. It hurt. The pain of missing my family was too much at times. I would get past my moment of grief and sit and think about how my family would be proud of me. I would think of what they would say, what they would actually feel knowing I was going to have a doctorate. Those thoughts bought a smile upon my tear-stained face. I wiped my tears and said, "Lord, help me, I've got work to do."

Sometimes in life when you've said all you can say, and prayed all you can pray, all you need do is stand, wait and listen. Then God will be your point of light to provide direction.

Prevailing

In the summer of 2018, I prepared to travel to Minneapolis, Minnesota to participate in my doctoral hooding and commencement ceremony. Reflecting on my last trip to Minnesota in 2010 to obtain my master's degree, I was blessed to have my sister with me at that commencement ceremony. This milestone was different — truly a bittersweet moment. I knew I would have moments of extreme happiness and moments of extreme sadness.

Preparing for the trip allowed me to reflect on my family. Every single day I thought, "Why can't my family be here to witness this great moment in my life?" I had anxiety thinking about the morning of graduation, just the anticipation and knowing how the day would go for me seeing the other happy graduates with their families and me knowing my family was not there physically.

I could not sleep the night before graduation, I tossed and turned all night, praying that God would let me have a great day and not let my emotions get the best of me. The morning of my graduation came. I got up, sat on the side of the bed and went into the other room where my friends were asleep. I smiled because I was grateful at that very moment for each of them. They did not complain about traveling across the world with me not once, but twice to attend my graduations. I then quietly shut the door.

I went back to sit on the side of my bed. I sat in silence. I thought of my undergraduate graduation. I remembered how proud Momma and Daddy were. None of us knew that was just the beginning for me academically. Here I was acquiring my third degree, but my life was incomplete. The ones that mattered the most were not there to physically celebrate with me.

I began to cry. My heart hurt so bad. I wanted my family there so bad. I began to pray and ask God to please take the pain away and allow me to enjoy the day that I had worked so hard to reach. I said a prayer and thanked

God for everything He had blessed me with, not knowing He had so much more in store for me. All I needed to do was trust Him and know He was God and He would never leave me.

I slowly got myself together before my friends woke up. When they woke up, they were excited, but sleepy, because we had to be at the venue early. Once we got in our van, we were ready for the day. That will be one of the most memorable days of my life. I did it! I had completed my doctoral journey. There were many late nights of reading, writing, crying, fussing, and cussing. At that very moment, it was all worth it. I was Dr. DaMesia D. Starling.

I can only hope I will inspire someone who is where I am from; who looks like me; who talks like me; to always dream big and achieve this level of academic success and beyond what is stereotypically slated to be above African Americans.

To have gone through the worst that any human could possibly go through, yet stand strong, and continue to strive for greatness is nothing short of prevailing.

Jeremiah 29:11 is one of my favorite scriptures. To know that God has a plan for me to prosper and not to harm me provides hope and keeps me wanting to move forward. I thank God daily for His will for my life.

Reflection

PERSONAL JOURNEY TO PREVAILING

Share your favorite Bible verse that helped you prevail.

_____

_____

_____

_____

_____

_____

_____

_____

_____

_____

_____

_____

_____

CHAPTER 5

PERSEVERANCE

{ *noun.* firm or obstinate continuance in a course of action in spite of difficulty or opposition. }

When my parents passed away, I knew I had to take care of myself and my sister. It is amazing that you gain strength when the only option you have is to be strong. My only choices were to adapt to my "new normal" or go insane. This new reality was the primary driving force to continue to strive for better. I knew the type of life I wanted for myself, and in a matter of two years, I came to the realization that I am/was my sister's sole provider.

In spite of all the heartbreaks I have experienced, I somehow continue to strive for greatness. I have a greater purpose now. I think about my parents with every accomplishment. I think about how proud they must be. I also chuckle a little just thinking of how excited they would be to see me as a Doctor and now a Dean at a college.

Thinking of perseverance, I am reminded of a story of a little girl who had a dance recital. The little girl cried the entire time while on stage. Although she cried and continued to do so, she never stopped dancing. Many people would have probably told the little girl to stop dancing, it is ok to stop. However, that is because many people feel crying is a weakness, I do not. As long as you do not let the tears stop you from obtaining the mission you are trying to obtain. So, if you are having a tough time, just remember to keep dancing through the tears and refer to the story of Job as I have countless times. Job was a faithful man, blameless and upright. He served God and was a diligent follower. Satan wanted to prove a point to God, that he could break man's will. So he asked if he could torture Job and God allowed it.

The only restriction God placed on Satan was he could not take Job's life. In the course of one day, Job was told by different servants that all his belongings and possessions, livestock and ten children had been killed or destroyed by natural disasters or thieves.

Despite all this, Job still praised God, even in his sorrow.

Next Job was afflicted with terrible skin sores and yet, he persevered and praised God. In his grieving and illness, Job's friends came and sat with him. Despite the terrible advice they offered him, Job still praised God. But soon his praises turned to questions, bitterness and anger.

Job questioned how a just God could allow such terrible things to happen, even to a faithful servant.

God eventually intervened and implored Job to be brave. Realizing the power of God and overcome by it, Job recognized God's true character and accepted his own faults and constraints as a human. Job also intervened for his friends and God had mercy on them, despite their horrible advice.

God then had mercy on Job and restored his health and all his possessions, granting him twice as much as he had previously, more children and a long prosperous life.

Job's story is the ultimate test of faith and example of perseverance in the Bible. Even in the darkest times, through death and turmoil, questions of

Perseverance

faith and God, Job was faithful and trusted God's plan.[1]

I believe this book will be a success if I can help just one person understand that everything that happens to you can work for your good, if you only let it. There were many times the devil meant for things to happen for bad. But I am so glad that God is a great God and will turn any traumatic, heart-wrenching, event to conclude in your favor. In my personal experience I knew I could not let my obstacles define me, and I never stopped believing that greater would be later for me. I couldn't and wouldn't rest until I realized my dream. You have to continue to believe that if you work hard and continue to push through, God will see you through and everything you've prayed for will come to pass.

I am continuously trying to make my life greater so that I can truly say I have left my mark and I was here. I have done things I never thought or imagined. I know God is continuing to keep me and I pray I continue to make my three angels proud.

Galatians 6:9 helps me push through any and all obstacles.

---

[1]: (wiscopts.net)

REFLECTION
WAYS I HAVE PERSEVERED

Share your favorite Bible verse that has helped you persevere.

___

___

___

___

___

___

___

___

___

___

___

___

CHAPTER 6

PEACEFUL

{ *adjective*. free from disturbance; tranquil. }

Prayer and my faith in God allowed me to overcome every mountain I have had to climb. I never asked God to remove the mountains, but I did ask Him to grant me the strength to climb them. With every stream of sweat and pain attributed to climbing up and over each mountain, my prayer life became stronger and more relevant. Through prayer, came peace. Prayer presented the knowledge that God will take care of me. God has always wrapped His arms around me to protect me not only from my enemies, but from myself. I need protection from myself when my thoughts consume my peace by overshadowing pain from the losses I have experienced.

The King James Bible uses the word *peace* in several different ways. *Peace* sometimes refers to a state of friendship between God and man. This peace between a holy God and sinful man has been affected by Christ's sacrificial death, "having made peace through the blood of his cross" (Colossians 1:20). In addition, as High Priest the Lord Jesus maintains that state of friendship on behalf of all who continue to "come to God by Him, seeing He always lives to make intercession for them" (Hebrews 7:25).

This state of friendship with God is a prerequisite for the second kind of peace, that which sometimes refers to a tranquil mind. It is only when "we have peace with God through our Lord Jesus Christ" (Romans 5:1) that we can experience the true peace of mind that is a fruit of the Holy Spirit. Peace then becomes His fruit exhibited in us (Galatians 5:22). Isaiah 26:3 tells us that God will keep us in "perfect peace" if our minds are "stayed" on Him, meaning our minds lean on Him, center on Him and trust in Him. Our tranquility of mind is "perfect" or imperfect to the degree that the "mind is stayed on" God rather than ourselves or on our problems.

Peace is experienced as we believe what the Bible says about God's nearness as in Psalm 139:1-12, and about His goodness and power, His mercy and love for His children, and His complete sovereignty over all of life's circumstances. But we can't trust someone we don't know, and it is crucial, therefore, to come to know intimately the Prince of Peace, Jesus Christ. Peace is experienced as a result of prayer. "Be anxious for nothing, but in everything by prayer and supplication, with thanksgiving, let your requests be made known to God; and the peace of God which surpasses all understanding, will guard your hearts and minds through Christ Jesus" (Philippians 4:6-7).

A peaceful mind and heart are experienced as a result of recognizing that an all-wise and loving Father has a purpose in our trials. "We know that all things work together for good to those who love God and are called according to His purpose" (Romans 8:28). God can bring a variety of good things, including peace, from the afflictions that we experience. Even the discipline and chastening of the Lord will "yield the peaceable fruit of righteousness" in our lives (Hebrews 12:11). They provide a fresh opportunity for "hoping in God" and eventually "praising Him" (Psalm 43:5). They help us "comfort" others when they undergo similar trials (2 Corinthians 1:4), and they "achieve for us an eternal glory that far outweighs them all" (2 Corinthians 4:17). Peace of mind and the tranquility of spirit that accompanies it are only available when we have true peace with God through the sacrifice of Christ on the cross in payment of our sins. Those who attempt to find peace in worldly pursuits will find themselves sadly deceived. For Christians, however, peace of mind is available through the intimate knowledge of, and complete trust in, the God who meets "all your needs according to his glorious riches in Christ Jesus" (Philippians 4:19).

I wouldn't say I am at peace 100%. There are days when my heartache is heavier than others. There are days when all I can do is cry and my heart aches for my family, just to have a phone call, or to have one last family dinner. To hear my daddy's loud laugh, to hear my momma's voice, or to see my sister's smile. I miss all those things and reliving their memories provides me with peace I never knew I could experience after losing them all. I smile when I think of how they are rejoicing together and watching over me and surrounding me with their love. I know they are always with me and although going through life without them is very hard, the memories we have shared will live on in my heart.

Through the grieving process, I had to grow: personally, spiritually, and emotionally. I had to continuously ask God to give me the courage to love with an open heart and not be closed off. I had started shutting family and friends out — not that I was depressed (or maybe I was and just didn't know it), but because I preferred to be alone.

I had to learn to ask God to allow me to accept the things I could not change, learn to change the things I had the power to change, and wisdom to know the difference. I had to learn to deal with the grieving myself and process how I wanted to live my "new life." It was hard but I was determined to not use anti-depressants or any mood stabilizers. I needed my pain to be raw and authentic so that I can move past it and learn to live again.

I have peace knowing that I have three guardian angels watching over me, protecting me.

We all know life can bring hectic and uncertain moments. When life gets me anxious or when I need some reassurance of God's love for me, I read Luke 1:78-79.

Reveal strategies you have used to help maintain and/or restore peace in your life.

Reflections

WAYS I ENSURED MY PEACE WAS MAINTAINED

Share your favorite Bible verse that helped you remain peaceful.

_____

_____

_____

_____

_____

_____

_____

_____

_____

_____

CHAPTER 7
PURPOSE

{ *noun.* the reason for which something is done or created or for which something exists. }

In life, you never know what your purpose is, until you find it. As a child, I knew I wanted to be an educator. I used to "play school" with my dolls. I remember writing on the walls of my closet and room as if they were my make-shift chalkboards. After graduating high school, I received my bachelor's degree in Education in 2003.

Through teaching, school leadership, district leadership and multiple roles in academia, I realized my purpose — reaching students. Even in my current role, I am able to reach students beyond the classroom. I am able to discuss future plans, prepare them for the teaching profession, and share my experiences in the education profession. I am able reach the students deeper due to me being an alumna of the college and actually graduating in the major in which I now teach. I am so humbled and honored to be here and give back to the place that provided my foundation.

Although I had to overcome various stumbling blocks, I do believe God does not put any more on us than we can bear. I am a true testimony. The stumbling blocks that were thrown at me, I stacked them and used them as steps to climb higher to reach goals that I personally set. I learned early on, the devil wants you to lie in your self-pity and give up. Only YOU can define your true destiny. It is my sincerest hope that I can inspire others so that they can know, you do not have to let your trials define you, prayer and perseverance is the key to obtaining your dreams. I have never felt sorry for myself; in fact, my work ethic has been strengthened by my adversity. God has a purpose for everything, we make plans, yet HE has the ultimate decision.

In life you never know what obstacles may be thrown your way, conversely you have control over how you handle them. I chose to be a conqueror and not allow my heartache, pain, and disappointments overtake who I am or aspire to become. Whatever God brings you to, he will bring you through.

I am ever grateful for the blessings that I am blessed with, through it all, I will continue to excel ...

I finally found my purpose.

Read and reflect on the following passage Job 42:2. Once read, write down and explore your thoughts about your life's purpose, your passions, and your joys.

Reflection

MY PURPOSE

Share your favorite Bible verse that allowed you
to outline a clear and precise purpose.

_____

_____

_____

_____

_____

_____

_____

_____

_____

_____

_____

_____

Chapter 8
PERSPECTIVE

{ *noun.* a particular attitude toward or way of regarding something; a point of view. }

On Monday, August 5, 2019, I was traveling home from work, like any other Monday. I arrived home to find my house was engulfed in flames. As I stood and saw the flames, I could not help but think, "God, what else do I have to lose?" The apartment home above mine was the root of the fire. The fire was so severe, the flames spread to five other units, including mine since my home was directly under the direct source of the fire.

After about three hours, I was able to enter my home to assess the damage and see what items could be salvaged. As I entered my home, I saw the damage from fire, smoke, and water. The firefighter walked me through the house as I tried to collect things that I needed since this was no longer my home. I packed as much as I could in a suitcase and headed to a hotel to think of what my next move would be.

After I checked into the hotel and sat on the bed after my nerves settled, I thanked God because it could have been worse. As bad as the fire was, no one was hurt, that was indeed a blessing. Although five families were displaced, we were still alive. I was drained, physically and emotionally. I talked to my best friend, then my aunt and uncle who came to the apartment as soon as they heard there was a fire. Each of them followed me to the hotel to ensure that I was okay. I am forever grateful to them for just being there.

The next morning, I had to gather myself, began making calls to my insurance company and began the quest to seek a new residence. I spent over a month in the hotel, having to start from scratch with buying furniture, appliances, TVs, linens, towels, and other random items that you don't expect to remember that need to be replaced. Through this period of starting over, I thought a lot about everything I went through with the deaths of my family members.

As I viewed the reality that I was having to rebuild my life from the fire, I had two thoughts. The first thought was, "Okay, this could be a good thing. Maybe this is needed so a fresh start can put the past behind me and I can think about the future blessings that God has for me." The second and most lingering thought was, "Why is this happening? I have lost everything possible and now this?" I had to immediately dismiss the second thought because I would always revert to sadness and that is not what I needed at that moment. I continually prayed and asked God to provide the strength that He had given me so many times before.

There were many days and nights I was frustrated with having to live in the hotel and having to go buy clothes or just needing things and not having what I needed because I no longer had a "home." I knew I was blessed, but the human side of me would become angry and frustrated. Admittedly, it became hard to remain positive. I knew I had to change my perspective on the "fire" situation. I needed to understand and remember that every trial and tribulation happened for a reason and although the situation was unexpected for me, God was right behind me every step of the way.

I knew the tears and hurt would work out for my good. I do believe with each tragedy I have encountered, I became stronger and wiser. There have been

Perspective

many times I felt like giving up, but I knew I couldn't. I had been through so many things that I did not understand, but I knew for everything there was a reason and I knew God had a way of turning everything around. I thought I lost a lot, but I gained so much more. I gained strength, courage, and wisdom. I was able to see the situation through this perspective because God had prepared me through other circumstances to use that perspective. He had developed that perspective in me.

Sometimes we need help to gain perspective on certain situations. Corinthians 4:17-18 is a passage that allowed me to focus on what was important. Please reflect and share insight on the things you had to put into perspective and how you went about doing so.

REFLECTION
IMPORTANT THINGS TO KEEP IN PERSPECTIVE

Share your favorite Bible verse that helped you keep priorities in perspective.

Made in the USA
Coppell, TX
27 May 2020